KETO

BREAD

MADE EASY

SIMPLE RECIPES

FUN AND HEALTHY KETO ALTERNATIVES!

Evelyn Portnoy

KETO BREAD

A COLLECTION OF EASY, TASTEFUL KETO BREAD RECIPES FOR THE ULTIMATE KETO COOKBOOK

By
Evelyn Portnoy
Copyright © by Wentworth Publishing House .

Published by
Savour Press, a DBA of Wentworth Publishing House

Let's get it started!

Welcome to Savour. Cooking brings family, friends, and classmates together in occasions where sumptuous foods are shared with. Whatever kind of recipes you prepare; it is always treasured by people close to you because you put more effort and do it with passion and love, just to please their impeccable taste buds. Preparing ketogenic foods for yourself or for anyone who are trying to lose weight seems difficult for you, especially when it comes to bread that are high in carbohydrates, but not anymore. Our main thrust is to let you enjoy ketogenic foods with the same savory taste of regular breads, sans carbohydrates and sugar, but high in healthy fats to keep you going. This is the gist of this cookbook, where we compiled 35 five-star bread recipes that use ingredients to let your body adapt to ketosis. Why get scared of bread, when you can have as many slices or servings as you want, with our recipes, nobody has the right to deprive you of this savory comfort food.

About This Book

Depriving yourself and your loved ones with delicious foods is no longer a scenario, now that there are many ways to prepare them without compromising your health, by substituting certain ingredients that is suitable to your dietary restrictions. If you are following a ketogenic diet, we at Savour is proud to introduce to you our 35 best bread recipes that detach from the regular recipes by not using flours that are so high in carbohydrates and sugars, but we replace them with coconut flour, almond flour, arrowroot flour, avocado oil, ghee, stevia, erythritol, almond milk, coconut milk, nutritional yeast flakes, ghee, psyllium husk powder, flax meal, and blended with zucchini, chia, rosemary to add flavor to your bread. We want to satisfy your carbohydrate cravings without wrecking your diet program with our collection of moist, creamylicious and comforting breads. That defines savory and healthy! Let's get ready to have a fun time!

VISIT US AT

www.savourypress.com

Also, by the editors at Savour Press's kitchen

The Chili Cookbook

The Quiche Cookbook

Indian Instant Pot Cookbook

The Cajun and Creole Cookbook

The Grill Cookbook

The Burger Book

The Ultimate Appetizers Cookbook

The West African Cookbook

Korean Seoul Cookbook

The Cast Iron Cookbook

The Holiday Cookbook

The Baking Book

The Crepe Cookbook

JOIN THE SAVOUR PRESS'S READERS CLUB AND RECEIVE A FREE COOKBOOK! JUST STAY UNTIL THE END OF THE BOOK AND CLICK ON THE BOOK OR LINK!

CONTENTS

INTRODUCTION

Get inspired by preparing our yummy and ketogenic-friendly breads that we specially collected for your satisfaction without depriving you the pleasures of eating, feel less guilty and you will ask for more slices. Most of our bread recipes are low carb, gluten-free, dairy free, nut free, Keto, Paleo, egg-free, grain-free, high in fiber, and sugar-free. Our collection of 35 bread recipes is excellent for people who are watching their diet, and great for hypertensive, diabetic and auto-immune sufferers. Don't doubt about our breads because they taste so good, and you can't even detect that they are Keto, the secret lies on the right measurement of substitute ingredients that we mentioned earlier. It starts with Nearly No Carb Keto Bread, Sesame Seed Keto Bread, Keto Cloud Bread - Low Carb Burger Buns, Sesame Seed Keto Bread, Keto Cloud Bread - Low Carb Burger Bunslower Naan Bread (Nut-free, Grain-free), Blueberry Loaf, Easy Almond Flax Keto Bread Recipe (Paleo & GF), and a lot more.

Enjoy!

Nearly No Carb Keto Bread

If you are avoiding carbohydrates and sugar, try this nearly no carbohydrate ketogenic bread. This is called this way as the bread has only 1 g carb, so nothing to worry when you have eaten one or two slices. This bread would take up to 31 minutes of your precious time.

Servings: 12

Ingredients

2 cups (210 grams) grated **mozzarella cheese**

8 ounces **cream cheese**

1/4 cup (27 grams) grated **parmesan cheese**

3 large **eggs**

1 tablespoon **baking powder**

1 cup (46 grams) crushed **cheese crisps**

Optional:

Herbs to taste

Spices to taste

DIRECTIONS:

Preheat the oven at 375°Fahrenheit.

Line a 12by17 jelly roll pan with parchment paper.

Put the mozzarella cheese and cream cheese in a large heat-proof bowl and microwave on high power for 1 minute.

Stir and microwave again for 1 minute and stir until the cheeses have totally melted.

Stir in cheese crisps, Parmesan cheese, baking powder, and egg until incorporated.

Spread the mixture evenly onto the pan.

Bake the break for fifteen to twenty minutes until the top part is lightly browned.

Let the pan cool on wire rack for fifteen minutes.

Remove the bread from baking pan and let cool on rack completely.

Slice bread into 12 pieces.

Serve!

Nutritional Information: 166 calories; 13 g fat (7 g saturated fat); 86 mg cholesterol; 294 mg sodium; 1 g carbohydrate; 0 g dietary fiber; 0 g total sugars; 9 g protein.

14

KETO POWERED Naan Bread (Nut-free, Grain-free)

This nut-free and grain-free naan bread offers a healthy alternative if you are on a restrictive diet due to an auto-immune disorder. It tastes so good without sugar, cheese, but it depends entirely on the fusion of arrowroot flour, avocado oil, garlic powder and mashed cauliflower florets.

Servings: 1

Ingredients

1/2 cup (64 grams) **arrowroot flour**

1 cup (140 grams) **cauliflower florets**

2 tablespoons **avocado oil** or **olive oil**

1 tablespoon (7 grams) **garlic powder**

Pinch of **salt** to taste

Directions

Preheat the oven at 450 Fahrenheit (230 C).

Fill a medium-size bowl with enough water and place the cauliflower.

Microwave the florets on high power until tender, checking every now and then to prevent burning.

Steam alternately the florets until tender crisps before placing in a food processor; process until the florets are mashed.

Combine in a bowl the cauliflower mash, arrowroot flour, avocado oil or olive oil, salt, and garlic powder.

Adjust the taste by adding salt and garlic powder according to your taste.

Mix the flour mixture until it becomes springy and press with your hands to turn the dough into flat bread.

Place the flat bread on the parchment paper-lined baking pan.

Bake for fifteen minutes until done. Let cool.

Enjoy!

Nutritional Information: 129 calorie; 3.8 g fat (0.8 g saturated fat); 0 mg cholesterol; 204 mg sodium; 21 g carbohydrate; 5.3 g dietary fiber; 4.5 g total sugars; 6.3 g protein.

Bread Rolls Recipe (Paleo, Keto, Egg-Free, Nut-Free)

This egg-free, nut-free, ketogenic and paleo bread rolls are perfect for your diet. In the absence of egg, create a gelatin egg by mixing the water with gelatin to let the coconut flour hold together. Its dense and dry textures are due to the coconut flour. Serve the bread rolls with ghee or coconut oil.

Servings: 2

Ingredients

6 tablespoons **coconut flour**

2 tablespoons melted **coconut oil**

1 tablespoon **Italian seasoning**

1/4 teaspoon **baking soda**

2 tablespoons **gelatin**

1/2 teaspoon **salt**

6 tablespoons **hot water**

Directions

Preheat the oven at 300 degrees Fahrenheit (150 C).

Combine in a large mixing bowl the coconut flour, coconut oil and baking soda.

Whisk in another bowl the hot water and gelatin to form gelatin egg. Stir gelatin egg into the flour mixture until incorporated.

Stir in the salt and Italian seasoning and combine thoroughly into dough.

Shape the dough into two small rolls and place on a baking tray lined earlier with parchment paper.

Bake the bread roll for forty to fifty minutes until the exterior part is crispy browned.

Let bread rolls cool completely to allow the gelatin to sit.

Serve!

Nutritional Information: 342 calorie; 20.2 g fat (15.1 g saturated fat); 5 g cholesterol; 756 mg sodium; 30.8 g carbohydrate; 18 g dietary fiber; 0.6 g total sugars; 12 g protein.

KETO CAROLINE CORNBREAD

This cornbread is specially created for health conscious individuals who are avoiding sugar and carbohydrates. It calls for coconut flour, coconut oil, eggs, apple cider vinegar and garlic powder to come up with aromatic and incredibly tasty bread for your snacks.

Servings: 10

Ingredients

2 tablespoons **apple cider vinegar**

4 **eggs**

1/2 cup **coconut flour**

1 cup **water**

1/4 cup melted **coconut oil**

1/2 teaspoon **garlic powder**

1/2 teaspoon **baking soda**

1/4 teaspoon **sea salt course**

Directions

Bring the eggs to room temperature and crack in the blender. Let the eggs sit for twenty minutes more.

Stir in the water,1/4 cup melted coconut oil and apple cider vinegar, make sure the oil is not too hot, to prevent the eggs from cooking.

Blend the ingredients on low speed for thirty seconds.

Stir in garlic powder, coconut flour, salt, and baking soda; blend for 1 minute.

Coat the baking tin or 2 small mini loaves with one teaspoon of coconut oil and fill with the batter.

Preheat the oven at 350 degrees F and bake for forty to forty-five minutes until done.

Note: You may also rub the surface of your bread with a teaspoon of coconut oil, one minute before taking out of your oven. Broil the cake on low temperature to achieve a pretty golden look.

Serve!

Nutritional Information: 98 calorie; 7 g fat (6 g saturated fat); 65 mg cholesterol; 151 mg sodium; 3 g carbohydrate; 2 g dietary fiber; 0 g total sugars; 3 g protein.

BACON JALAPEÑO BREAD

Enjoy a hefty snack by preparing this Keto bread consisting of bacon and jalapeños. They are great for your breakfast or brunch with your favorite juice drinks. The nutritional info provided is based on four servings.

Servings: 4-6

Ingredients

4 ounces turkey **bacon** (about 4 thick slices)

6 large **eggs**

3 large **jalapeños**

1 tablespoon **ghee** for greasing

1/2 cup melted **ghee**

1/2 cup **coconut flour**

¼ teaspoon **baking soda**

1/2 teaspoon **sea salt**

1/4 cup **water**

Directions

Preheat the oven at 400 degrees F.

Prepare the jalapeños by slicing and place on a baking tray with the bacon slices. Roast for ten minutes, flipping midway until done.

Slightly cool and remove seeds of jalapeño before placing both in the food processor; pulsing thoroughly until smooth.

Combine in a large bowl the ghee, water and egg; sift the coconut flour, baking soda and sea salt.

Fold the jalapeño-bacon mixture into the flour mixture and place in a greased 1.5 quart loaf pan.

Bake the bread for forty to forty-five minutes until there is no more batter left in a toothpick after removing from the center of the bread.

Let cool for ten to fifteen minutes and slice.

Serve!

Nutritional Information: 339 calorie; 22.6 g fat (8.3 g saturated fat); 315 mg cholesterol; 1074 mg sodium; 11.6 g carbohydrate; 6.3 g dietary fiber; 0.9 g total sugars; 22.1 g protein.

Cinnamon Bread (grain-free, nut-free, sugar-free & low-carb)

Prepare a sumptuous brunch by including this Keto cinnamon bread sweetened with stevia. If you are lactose intolerant, use coconut oil and coco milk with 1/8 teaspoon of salt. Add two tablespoons of coco sugar or raw honey to the batter if you are using a natural sweetener.

Servings: 10

Ingredients

1/2 teaspoon **baking soda**

1/2 cup **coconut flour**

1 teaspoon **cinnamon**

1/2 teaspoon **baking powder**

3 pastured **eggs**

1/4 teaspoon **Stevia** or sweetener of choice

1/3 cup **pure sour cream** or **Greek Yogurt**

1 teaspoon **vinegar**

2 tablespoons **water**

3 tablespoons **salted butter**

Directions

Preheat the oven at 350 degrees Fahrenheit.

Coat the loaf pan with cooking oil and place a parchment paper on the bottom of your baking pan.

Whisk all dry ingredients until blended well.

Whisk in the remaining ingredients and adjust the sweetness by adding more stevia if desired.

Let mixture stand for three minutes and blend once more.

Spread the batter in the loaf pan and bake for twenty-five to thirty minutes until done. Let cool on wire rack.

Serve!

Nutritional Information: 93 calorie; 7 g fat (4 g saturated fat); 77 mg cholesterol; 111 mg sodium; 5 g carbohydrate; 2.5 g dietary fiber; 0 g total sugars; 2.9 g protein.

Keto Flatbread Recipe with Nutritional Yeast

This Middle Eastern bread is loaded with nutritional yeast that surely will become a big hit for health buffs. It is high in dietary fiber and it uses almond milk, almond flour and coconut milk plus Italian seasoning to boost its natural flavor.

Servings: 6

Ingredients

1 tablespoon **dried instant yeast** or **nutritional yeast flakes**

1/2 cup **unsweetened almond milk**

1 cup **almond flour**

1 1/2 cup **coconut flour**

1 tablespoon **garlic powder**

2 teaspoons **baking powder**

Dash of salt and pepper

1 teaspoon **Italian seasoning**

2 **egg whites**

1 **whole egg**

Directions

Preheat the oven at 320 degrees Fahrenheit (160 C).

Place the almond milk in a heat-proof bowl and microwave for forty-five seconds and whisk in nutritional yeast.

Slightly cool and sprinkle with natural sweetener to activate or add more nutritional yeast flakes for better results.

Combine in a separate bowl the almond flour, coco flour, garlic powder, baking powder, salt, pepper, and Italian seasoning.

29

When the almond milk is cooled, whisk in the whole egg and the egg whites; pour into the flour mixture and mix with a wooden spoon until incorporated.

Divide the batter into six equal portions and form into dough balls.

Flatten out the dough balls into a one-half-inch thick flat oval shape.

Bake the bread for twelve to fifteen minutes.

Serve!

Nutritional Information: 217 calorie; 4 g net carbs; 3 g total sugars; 12 g fat; 14 g carbohydrate; 10 g dietary fiber; 11 g protein.

Keto Graham Cracker Bread Recipe

Tired of eating the same grocery-bought crackers that are salty, oily and sugary? This Keto cracker recipe uses flax meal, almond flour and cinnamon powder for flavoring. It is sweetened with erythritol and its creamy texture is courtesy of melted ghee and egg.

Servings: 8 (24 cracker bread)

Ingredients

2 tablespoons **flax meal**

2 cups **almond flour**

1/2 tablespoon **cinnamon powder**

1/4 cup **erythritol**

1 whisked large **egg**

1 teaspoon **baking powder**

Dash of **salt**

3 tablespoons melted **ghee**

Directions

Preheat the oven at 350 degrees Fahrenheit (175 C).

Combine all ingredients in a large mixing bowl until they come together as dough.

Thinly roll the dough on a parchment paper, scoring with a pizza cutter to form into 2x2-inch squares.

Poke with a fork on top of each square nicely for decoration purposes.

Place the parchment paper onto a greased baking tray.

Bake the crackers for eight to ten minutes until evenly browned. Let cool.

Serve!

Nutritional Information: 199 calorie; 2 g net carbs; 1 g total sugars; 18 g fat; 6 g carbohydrate; 4 g dietary fiber; 6 g protein.

CHEESY FLAX & CHIA SEED CRACKER BREAD (LOW CARB AND GLUTEN-FREE)

Love the taste of this nutty and crunchy gluten-free and low carb Keto cracker bread. It is loaded with flax and chia seeds, which is high in nutritional value. Its cheesy taste is appealing even for non-Keto followers.

Servings: 28-30 cracker breads

Ingredients

2 tablespoons **chia seeds**

1 1/2 cups **ground flax seeds**

1/2 c **shredded extra sharp cheddar**

2 well beaten **eggs**

1/2 teaspoon **salt**

1/2 teaspoon **garlic powder**

1/2 teaspoon **pepper**

Directions

Combine in a large mixing bowl, all ingredients using your hands to form thick dough.

Coat with nonstick spray a sheet of plastic wrap or foil.

Shape the dough into log and place on the greased foil or plastic wrap.

Roll the dough at least one ruler long with a 1 ½ inch diameter. It is up to you if you want it round, or form into squares.

Place the dough in the freezer for five minutes until hardened.

Preheat the oven to 350 degrees F and slice the cold dough about 1/4-1/2-inch thick slices.

Place the dough slices flat on the greased cookie sheet.

Bake for twelve to fifteen minutes until nicely browned.

Remove cracker bread from oven. Let cool.

Enjoy!

Nutritional Information: 40 calorie; 2.3 g fat (0.4 g saturated fat); 0 mg cholesterol; 51 mg sodium; 2.3 g carbohydrate; 2 g dietary fiber; 0.1 g total sugars; 0.1 g total sugars; 1.7 g protein.

KETO FLATBREAD RECIPE – GLUTEN-FREE, LOW CARB

People with special diet, should try this Keto flatbread, which is free from gluten and low in carbohydrates. It is perfect as a side dish, appetizer and snack. It is stuffed with spinach and can be finished in 22 minutes only.

Servings: 6

Ingredients

1 tablespoon **cream cheese**

3/4 cup **shredded low moisture mozzarella cheese**

2 tablespoons **almond flour**

1 **egg**

1/8 teaspoon **garlic powder**

1/4 cup cooked and drained **spinach**

Salt to taste

Directions

Preheat oven at 350 degrees Fahrenheit.

Place cream cheese and mozzarella cheese in a microwave-safe bowl and melt in thirty-second bursts, stirring to mix together in every interval.

Remove from microwave and combine with almond flour, spinach and egg.

Flatten out the batter on the surface of your baking sheet lined with a sheet of parchment paper.

Sprinkle 1/8 teaspoon garlic powder and a pinch of salt on top.

Bake the bread for fifteen minutes, flip and bake for five minutes more until both sides are crisp and browned.

Enjoy!

Nutritional Information: 75 calorie; 5 g fat (2 g saturated fat); 37 mg cholesterol; 111 mg sodium; 1 g carbohydrate; 5 g protein.

Coconut Flour Flatbread

This flatbread calls for five ingredients and can be done quickly. Combine all ingredients and divide into two to form a round flat shape. You may double the ingredients as your housemates will ask for another serving.

Servings: 2 coconut flatbreads

Ingredients

1 tablespoon melted **coconut** oil

1/4 teaspoon **baking powder**

1 1/2 tablespoons **coconut flour**

1/8 teaspoon **sea salt**

1 **egg**

Directions

Preheat the oven at 350 degrees F.

Combine in a large bowl the coconut flour, baking powder and sea salt and mix thoroughly.

Add the melted coconut oil and egg; mix well until incorporated.

Let sit for several minutes until the liquid is absorbed by the flour.

Fill the baking pan with half of the batter and spread using a rubber spatula to form into a circle with the size of a bun.

Do the same steps for the remaining half of the batter.

Bake the flatbread for ten minutes until golden brown.

Serve!

Nutritional Information: 117 calorie; 7.8 g fat (3.2 g saturated fat); 82 mg cholesterol; 191 mg sodium; 8 g carbohydrate; 4.5 g dietary fiber; 0.2 g total sugars; 4.3 g protein.

LOW CARB FLATBREAD

This low carbohydrate flatbread is ideally the best if you are on a restricted diet as it is sugarless, gluten-free and only uses coconut flour, almond flour and unflavored whey protein powder. This is an excellent recipe in making Panini or a sandwich.

Servings: 10

Ingredients

6 tablespoons **coconut flour**

3 1/4 cups **almond flour**

2 teaspoons **baking powder**

1/3 cup **unflavored whey protein powder**

1/2 teaspoon **salt**

1/2 teaspoon **garlic powder**

1/4 cup **avocado oil** or **olive oil**

4 large **eggs**

1/4 cup **water**

Directions

Preheat the oven at 325 degrees F.

Whisk in a large bowl the coconut flour, almond flour, baking powder, salt, garlic and whey protein until well blended.

Whisk in water, oil and eggs until all ingredients form into sticky dough.

Place the dough onto a large sheet of parchment paper, patting the dough into a rough rectangular piece.

Place on top with another sheet of parchment paper.

Roll the dough into a rough rectangle with ½- inch to ¾-inch thickness.

Place the dough on a large baking sheet; remove the top layer of paper.

Bake for twenty minutes until a bit firm. Remove immediately from oven and cool before slicing.

With a sharp bread knife, cut the bread into ten parts and cut through its bready center into two halves enough to fill with sandwich fillings.

Serve!

Nutritional Information: 316 calorie; 25.9 g fat; 6.1 g net carbs; 11 g total carbohydrates; 5.4 g dietary fiber; 13.2 g protein.

KETO ZUCCHINI BREAD RECIPE

This vegetarian Keto zucchini bread can fill your hunger with its dense texture and flavorful taste. Each slice of this bread is a mixture of zucchini, coco flour, almond flour, coco oil, and eggs. It has no sugar or natural sweetener added, so your diabetic diet is not compromised at all.

Servings: 10 slices

Ingredients

1 large shredded **zucchini**

4 medium **eggs**

1/4 cup of **coconut flour**

1/2 cup of **almond flour**

1 teaspoon of **vanilla extract**

1 teaspoon of **baking powder**

8 tablespoons of **coconut oil**

Dash of **salt**

Directions

Prepare the zucchini by squeezing out extra moisture, set aside.

Preheat your oven at 350 degrees Fahrenheit (175 C).

Combine all the ingredients in a large bowl until incorporated. Pour the batter into a loaf pan.

Bake for fifty minutes, let cool and slice before serving.

Enjoy!

Nutritional Information: 162 calorie; 1 g net carbs; 1 g total sugars; 15 g fat; 3 g carbohydrates; 2 g dietary fiber; 4 g protein.

KETO "CORNBREAD" MUFFINS RECIPE

This is the simplest way to prepare a Keto cornbread muffin by combining all ingredients and place in a greased muffin pan. The cornbread is flavored with ghee and its creaminess is due to the blend of coconut milk, eggs with coconut flour and almond flour.

Servings: 6

Ingredients

¼ cup **coconut flour**

¾ cup **almond flour**

1 teaspoon **salt**

2 teaspoons **baking powder**

½ cup **coconut milk**

3 **eggs**

2 tablespoons **ghee**

Directions

Preheat oven at 350 degrees F (177 C).

Coat the bottom and sides of muffin pan with coconut oil or line with muffin liners.

Combine all ingredients in a large mixing bowl and pour into the greased muffin pan.

Bake for twenty minutes.

Serve!

Nutritional Information: 191 calorie; 2 g net carbs; 1 g total sugars; 17 g fat; 5 g carbohydrate; 3 g dietary fiber; 6 g protein.

KETO ALMOND BREAD

Treat your loved ones with this vegetarian Keto bread filled with eggs, almond flour, and olive oil and mustard powder. You also have the option to include the optional yeast mixture by combining the gluten-free instant yeast with tepid water to enhance its flavor.

Servings: 4

Ingredients

2 **whisked eggs**

1 1/2 teaspoons of **baking powder**

1 cup **almond flour**

1 teaspoon **fine salt**

1 teaspoon **mustard powder**

3 tablespoons of **olive oil**

Optional yeast mixture:

1 teaspoon **gluten-free instant yeast**

1 tablespoon **tepid water**

Directions

Preheat the oven at 350 degrees F (180 C).

Combine in a large mixing bowl the whisked eggs, baking powder, almond flour, salt, olive oil and mustard powder.

You may also add the optional yeast mixture by combining the yeast with the water.

Mix the ingredients thoroughly to form sticky dough.

Grease a 9cmby20cm or a 3 ½-inch by 8-inch baking tin and spread the batter evenly.

Bake the batter for half an hour.

When done, tip out and slice the bread into four thick slices.

Serve!

Nutritional Information: 257 calorie; 2 g net carbs; 1 g total sugars; 24 g fat; 5 g carbohydrate; 3 g dietary fiber; 8 g protein.

TEN-MINUTE KETO TOAST RECIPE (GLUTEN-FREE, LOW-CARB)

Elevate your impeccable taste buds by having this Keto bread done in ten-minutes with five ingredients only. Place all bread ingredients in a mug, microwave and slice before toasting in the oven for several minutes. Your bread is ready to serve.

Servings: 2

Ingredients

1/2 teaspoon **baking powder**

1/3 cup **almond flour**

1 **whisked egg**

2 ½ tablespoons **melted ghee**

1/8 teaspoon **salt**

Directions

Preheat oven at 400 degrees F (200 C).

Combine all the bread ingredients in a mug until incorporated and microwave on high power for ninety seconds. Let cool for a few minutes.

Pop out the bread from the mug; cut into four bread slices.

Place the bread slices onto a greased baking tray; toast for four minutes until golden brown.

Serve with ghee.

Enjoy!

Nutritional Information: 270 calorie; 1 g net carbs; 1 g total sugars; 27 g fat; 3 g carbohydrate; 2 g dietary fiber; 6 g protein.

Keto Loaf of Bread [Gluten-Free, Dairy-Free]

This soft and light bread loaf is a perfect way to show your love to your family. It is not only a healthy alternative, but surely they will enjoy its creamy taste, especially if you serve it with their favorite sandwich spread.

Servings: 12

Ingredients

3 tablespoons **whey protein powder**

3 cups **almond flour**

1/4 cup canned **coconut milk**

1/2 cup plus 2 tablespoons **coconut oil**

2 teaspoons **baking powder**

3 **whisked eggs**

1/4 teaspoon **salt**

1 tablespoon **Italian seasoning**

1 teaspoon **baking soda**

Directions

Preheat oven at 300 degrees F (150 C).

Coat a 9by5-inch loaf pan with coconut oil or olive oil.

Combine the bread ingredients in a large mixing bowl.

Fill the pan with the batter and evenly spread out with a spatula.

Bake the batter for one hour. Let cool and flip until nicely golden.

Cut the bread into slices using a bread knife.

Serve!

Nutritional Information: 260 calorie; 2 g net carbs; 1 g total sugars; 25 g fat; 5 g carbohydrate; 3 g dietary fiber; 7 g protein.

BLUEBERRY LOAF

This healthy loaf bread is loaded with heavy cream, coconut flour, almond flour, eggs and wild blueberries. It is flavored with vanilla and sweetened with truvia. In this recipe, you need 7 tablespoons of truvia, which is equivalent to one cup of sugar. You have the option to use muffin tins or loaf pan.

Servings: 8 slices or 24 mini muffins

Ingredients

1 tablespoon **coconut flour**

1 1/2 cups **almond flour**

7 tablespoons **truvia**

1 1/2 teaspoons **baking powder**

4 tablespoons **heavy cream**

3 tablespoons **oil**

2 **eggs**

1 teaspoon **vanilla**

100 grams **wild blueberries**

Directions

Preheat oven at 300 degrees F.

Whisk in a large bowl the coconut flour, almond flour, 6 tablespoons of truvia, and baking powder.

Whisk in another bowl the vanilla, heavy cream and oil.

Fold the cream mixture with the flour mixture with a whisk until the batter becomes thicker.

Wash blueberries and stir in 1 tablespoon of truvia.

Place the blueberries on the surface of the batter and slowly combine into the batter.

Prepare a loaf pan by lining with a sheet of parchment paper. Evenly spread the batter on the pan.

Bake bread for 1 hour and ten minutes, turning the loaf pan midway. Let bread cool in the pan.

If you prefer mini muffins, bake the batter at 350 degrees for ten to thirteen minutes until the surface is golden brown.

Enjoy!

Nutritional Information: 221 calories; 20 g fat; 4 net carbs; 7 g protein; 7 g carbohydrate; 3 g dietary fiber.

Easy Almond Flax Keto Bread Recipe (Paleo & GF)

This recipe can benefit both Keto and Paleo followers as it is loaded with a powerful flavor with the absence of sugar. You may omit the honey if you are on the ketogenic diet. Anyways, it still tastes so good with its crunchy crust and chewy, buttery texture to satiate your sweet cravings.

Servings: 8

Ingredients

1/4 cup **ground flax seeds**

1 1/2 cups **blanched almond flour**

1/2 teaspoon **sea salt**

1 tablespoon **whole flax seeds**

4 beaten large **eggs**

1/2 teaspoon **baking soda**

2 teaspoons **honey** (optional- omit this for Keto)

1/2 teaspoon **apple cider vinegar**

1 tablespoon **butter or oil** for greasing

Directions

Preheat the oven at 300° F.

Combine in a large mixing bowl, all ingredients, excluding the butter for greasing, until completely mixed.

Coat with butter an 8-inch or 9-inch loaf pan and spread the dough evenly.

Bake for forty-five minutes until done. Let bread cool completely before serving.

Serve!

Nutritional Information: 196 calorie; 16 g fat (2 g saturated fat); 85 mg cholesterol; 269 mg sodium; 6 g carbohydrate; 3 g dietary fiber; 3 g dietary fiber; 8 g protein.

KETO NUT AND SEED BREAD RECIPE

This nutty bread recipe is not only yummy to eat, but it is very simple to do by combining all ingredients and bake. Its nutty texture is a blend of whole almonds, hazelnuts, chia seeds, raw pecans, pumpkin seeds, poppy seeds, and sunflower seeds. Nothing to worry the seeds and nuts are Keto-friendly.

Servings: 15 slices

Ingredients

1/2 cup **whole almonds**

1/2 cup **almond flour**

1/2 cup **hazelnuts**

1 cup **raw pecans**

1/2 cup **chia seed**

1/2 cup **flax meal**

1 cup **sunflower seeds**

4 **whisked eggs**

1 cup **pumpkin seeds**

6 tablespoons of **olive oil**

1/4 cup **poppy seeds**

1 tablespoon **lemon juice**

1 teaspoon **salt**

Directions

Preheat the oven at 350 degrees F (175 C).

Combine all bread ingredients until incorporated and spread into a greased loaf pan.

Bake for forty-five minutes until the toothpick comes out without traces of batter after removing from the center of the bread.

Enjoy!

Nutritional Information: 316 calorie; 1 g total sugars; 28 g fat; 11 g carbohydrate; 5 g dietary fiber; 11 g protein; 6 g net carbs.

Easy Keto Almond Coconut Bread Recipe

This bread has reached its perfection due to the blend of melted ghee, eggs, flax meal, eggs, coconut flour and almond flour. Its moist texture is ideal for your midnight snack, brunch or breakfast. This is easy to make by combining all ingredients and bake.

Servings: 12

Ingredients

6 **whisked eggs**

1/2 cup **melted ghee**

1/4 cup **coconut flour**

3/4 cup **almond flour**

1 teaspoon **baking powder**

2 tablespoons **flax meal**

Dash of salt

Directions

Preheat oven at 350 degrees F (175 C).

Combine all ingredients in a large mixing bowl, stir until incorporated.

Pour the mixture into a greased 9x5-inch baking pan.

Bake for thirty-five to forty minutes until there is no more batter left in a toothpick after removing from center of bread. Let cool before serving.

Enjoy!

Nutritional Information: 159 calorie; 0 g total sugars; 15 g fat; 3 g carbohydrate; 1 g net carbs; 2 g dietary fiber; 5 g protein.

KETO AVOCADO CHOCOLATE BREAD RECIPE

This Keto bread is loaded with nutrients, but it is high in calorie. A piece of advice, just limit your serving to 1 slice if you are on a diet program as it can affect your weight loss program, though the bread is sweetened with stevia.

Servings: 8

Ingredients

3 tablespoons **coconut oil**

2 mashed **ripe avocados**

2 cups **almond flour**

3 **whisked eggs**

1 teaspoon **baking soda**

1/2 cup **cacao powder**

1 teaspoon **vanilla extract**

Dash of **salt**

1/2 teaspoon **baking powder**

Stevia to taste

Directions

Preheat oven to 350 degrees Fahrenheit (175 C).

Mix in a large bowl, all ingredients and place in a greased loaf pan.

Bake the batter for forty to forty-five minutes until done. Let cool completely in pan.

Slice before serving.

Serve!

Nutritional Information: 309 calorie; 5 g net carbs; 1 g total sugars; 26 g fat; 13 g carbohydrate; 8 g dietary fiber; 10 g protein.

Keto Dinner Rolls Recipe

These nutritious dinner rolls are what you need for your ketosis needs. Each roll is loaded with psyllium husk powder, which aids in the detoxification process as it can cleanse your colon, and improves liver, heart and pancreas functions.

Servings: 9 bread rolls

Ingredients

1/4 cup **almond flour**

1/3 cup **coconut flour**

1 teaspoon **baking powder**

1/4 cup **psyllium husk powder**

Dash of **garlic powder**

1 teaspoon **baking soda**

4 large **eggs**

Dash of **salt**

1/4 cup **water**

2 teaspoons **olive oil**

1/4 cup **ghee**

Directions

Preheat the oven at 350 degrees F (175 C).

Mix in a large bowl the almond flour, psyllium husk powder, coconut flour, baking powder, garlic powder, baking soda, and salt, until well blended.

Whisk the eggs in a separate bowl together with the water and olive oil.

Whisk in melted ghee, make sure it is not hot.

Fold the egg mixture to the flour mixture; stir to combine fully. Let sit for five minutes until the batter becomes a little firm.

Shape the dough into nine balls of the same size.

Place the dough balls on a small tray lined with a sheet of parchment paper.

Bake for twenty-five to thirty minutes.

During the last ten minutes of baking time, reduce oven temperature to 300 degrees F.

Let cool on a wire rack. Store bread rolls in an airtight food container.

Enjoy!

Nutritional Information: 149 calorie; 1 g net carbs; 1 g total sugars; 12 g fat; 5 g carbohydrate; 4 g dietary fiber; 5 g protein.

Multi Seed Bagels Low-carb and Gluten Free

Dubbed as the ultimate Keto bagel, these bagels are what you need if you can't live without carbs. Each bagel has low carb and gluten-free. It calls for psyllium fiber, coconut flour, hemp hearts, aluminum-free baking powder with the addition of sesame seeds, pumpkin seeds and seasoned with Celtic sea salt.

Servings: 6 small bagels

Ingredients

1/4 cup **psyllium fiber**

1 cup **coconut flour**

1/2 cup **hemp hearts**

1/2 cup **sesame seeds**

6 **organic egg whites**

1/2 cup **pumpkin seeds**

1 tablespoon **aluminum-free baking powder**

1 teaspoon **Celtic sea salt**

Directions

Preheat the oven at 350 degrees Fahrenheit.

Combine in a large mixing bowl, all dry ingredients, stir to blend well.

Put the egg whites in a blender and process until extra foamy; pour into the dry ingredients and stir to incorporate, until crumbly.

Pour one cup of boiling water to the mixture, stirring often, until the dough is smooth yet crumbly and easy to handle.

Form the dough into a large ball and shape it into six equal-size balls.

Prepare a cookie sheet by lining with a sheet of parchment paper. Hold each dough ball in your hand and make a hole by sticking your thumb through it.

Place the dough onto the cookie sheet and form them into six small bagels, pressing lightly with your fingers.

Sprinkle on top with poppy or sesame seeds. Bake the bagels for fifty-five minutes.

Turn off the oven and let cool inside for added crunch on the surface.

Serve!

Nutritional Information: 352 calorie; 19 g fat; 8 g carbohydrate; 20 g dietary fiber; 18 g protein.

ROSEMARY COCONUT SAVOURY BREAD

Indulge yourself with this savory bread made of flax meal, coconut flour and coconut milk. It is oozing with aroma with the inclusion of freshly ground rosemary, eggs, and olive oil with baking soda and seasoned with sea salt.

Servings: 10 slices

Ingredients

1/4 cup **olive oil**

4 **whole eggs**

1 teaspoon **freshly ground rosemary**

1/4 cup **coconut milk**

1 teaspoon **coarse sea salt**

1 teaspoon **baking soda**

3/4 cup **coconut flour**

1/3 cup **flax meal**

Directions

Preheat oven at 180 degrees C (350F).

Using a hand mixer beat in a bowl the whole eggs, rosemary and coconut milk until smooth.

Beat in the soda, sea salt, flax meal and coconut flour, stir until well blended and the mixture is a bit dry.

Using a spatula, scrap the dough into a greased heat-proof dish, and form into a bread shape or scoop the dough into small baking tin and evenly spread out using a rubber spatula.

Bake for forty-five minutes until done.

Enjoy!

Nutritional Information: 135 calorie; 10.5 g fat (3.2 g saturated fat); 65 mg cholesterol; 343 mg sodium; 7.6 g carbohydrate; 4.9 g dietary fiber; 0.3 g total sugars; 4.4 g protein.

KETO-ADAPTED BREAD

This Keto-Adapted bread has only three ingredients, the eggs, onion powder and unflavored egg white protein. Substitute the egg white protein if it is not available with ¾ to one cup of whey protein.

Servings: 18 slices

Ingredients

12 **eggs**, separated

½ teaspoon **onion powder** (optional)

½ cup **Jay Robb unflavored egg white protein** (or ¾ to 1 cup **whey protein**)

Directions

Preheat the oven at 325 degrees Fahrenheit.

Separate the whites and yolks.

Reserve the yolk and whip the egg whites with a stand mixer for a few minutes until stiff.

Slowly combine the egg white protein powder with the egg whites.

Gently fold the yolk into the egg whites, be careful not to fall the whites.

Coat the bread pan with coconut oil spray.

Fill the pan with the mixture and bake for twenty-five minutes to thirty minutes until it turns golden brown.

Let bread cool fully to prevent falling apart when slicing.

Slice and serve.

Enjoy!

Nutritional Information: 49 calorie; 2.9 g fat; 0.5 g carbohydrate; 5.2 g protein; trace fiber (53.5% fat, 42.5% protein, 4% carbs).

THANKSGIVING BREAD

Who says you can't celebrate Thanksgiving with Keto bread? This bread recipe proves them wrong as it follows the ketogenic diet by using coconut flour, ghee and almond flour. The bread is nutty, crunchy and aromatic with the blend of spices, herbs, walnuts, eggs and bacon.

Servings: 10 slices

Ingredients

1 chopped **onion**

1 tablespoon **ghee**

½ cup roughly chopped **walnuts**

2 chopped **stalks celery**

½ cup **coconut flour**

1½ cups **almond flour**

¼ teaspoon **salt**

1 teaspoon **baking soda**

1 tablespoon finely chopped **fresh rosemary**

2 tablespoons finely **chopped sage**

4 **eggs**

Pinch of **freshly grated nutmeg**

2 to 3 **cooked and crumbled bacon strips**

½ cup **chicken broth** or **turkey broth**

Directions

Preheat oven at 350 degrees F.

Place the ghee in a skillet and melt on medium heat.

Stir-fry the onion and celery in melted ghee for five minutes.

Add walnuts and stir-fry until tender, set aside mixture.

Combine in a large mixing bowl the coconut flour, baking soda, almond flour, nutmeg, salt, rosemary and sage. Stir to incorporate.

Add the onion mixture to the flour mixture together with the chicken broth and eggs, mix until well blended.

Fold the bacon into the batter.

Grease a loaf pan and evenly spread the batter.

Bake for thirty-five to forty-five minutes until the toothpick comes out without traces of batter.

Enjoy!

Nutritional Information: 220 calorie; 17 g fat (3.5 g saturated fat); 75 mg cholesterol; 355 mg sodium; 9.7 g carbohydrate; 5.1 g dietary fiber; 1.3 g total sugars; 10.1 g protein.

Keto Sandwich Bread

Dieters should try preparing their Ketogenic sandwich by following this simple recipe. The sandwich bread contains flaxseed meal, almond flour, walnut oil and sunflower seeds. If stevia is unavailable, you can substitute it with honey, but this is optional.

Servings: 2 individual breads

Ingredients

4 tablespoons **flaxseed meal**

3/4 cup **almond flour**

1 1/2 teaspoons **baking powder**

2 tablespoons **toasted sunflower seeds**

3 **eggs**

1/4 teaspoon **kosher salt** or **sea salt**

1 1/2 tablespoons **walnut oil**

1 teaspoon **honey** (optional)

Butter or **oil** for greasing

Directions

Prepare the sunflower seeds by crushing with a rolling pin or heavy thing; make sure not to pulverize the seeds to add nutty texture to your bread.

Combine in a medium-sized bowl, all dry ingredients.

Whisk in another bowl the eggs along with walnut oil and pour into the dry ingredients, stir to combine well.

Divide the batter into two ramekins.

Cook the bread one at a time in the microwave for one minute and twenty seconds.

Note: When preparing sandwiches, trim off the rounded part of the bread to come up with flat sandwiches. Recycle the trimmings and freeze, by using them as grain-free breadcrumbs for your next cooking.

Enjoy!

Nutritional Information: 317 calorie; 22.9 g fat (4.6 g saturated fat); 251 mg cholesterol; 409 mg sodium; 12.6 g carbohydrate; 5.7 g dietary fiber; 3.7 g total sugars; 15.2 g protein.

Sesame Seed Keto Bread

While you can't do away with bread, this recipe calls for sesame seed flour, butter, eggs with baking powder so that you can enjoy a slice of bread without dairy, free of gluten, low carb, nut free, vegetarian and Keto/paleo rolled into one. This is perfect for your new diet regimen.

Servings: 8

Ingredients

7 large **eggs**

2 cups **sesame seed flour**

1 teaspoon **baking powder**

1/2 melted cup **butter**

Directions

Preheat your oven at 180 degree C (355 F).

Separate the egg whites from egg yolks in a large mixing bowl; beat the whites with a hand mixer until fluffy and white.

Combine in another bowl the egg yolk, baking powder, sesame seed flour and melted butter.

Slowly fold the egg yolk mixture into the beaten egg whites.

Mix together until it reaches uniform color. Line a bread loaf tin pan with baking paper.

Fill the pan with the batter and bake for forty-five minutes until the center is done.

Serve!

Nutritional Information: 368 calorie; 30 g fat (11 g saturated fat); 217 mg cholesterol; 227 mg sodium; 10 g carbohydrate; 8 g dietary fiber; 0.3 g total sugars; 17 g protein.

Keto Cloud Bread - Low Carb Burger Buns

Introducing ketosis in your system could be difficult if you can't live without carbohydrate. This light and fluffy bread recipe called as cloud bread works well on your diet program. This is good for you because it is low carb, gluten-free, Keto, nut free and vegetarian with only 4 to five ingredients needed.

Servings: 8

Ingredients

1/2 teaspoon **cream of tartar**

4 large **eggs**

1/2 teaspoon **salt**

1/4 cup **cream cheese**

Optional:

1/2 teaspoon **garlic powder**

Directions

Separate the egg whites from the egg yolks.

Whisk in a bowl all egg whites using an electric mixer for one to two minutes until fluffy and whitish.

Whisk in cream of tartar for 1 minute more until it forms a soft peak.

Combine in another bowl the cream cheese, garlic powder and egg yolks and whisk on high speed until incorporated.

Slowly fold the egg yolk-cream cheese mixture into the egg whites, whisk until well blended.

Prepare the baking tray by lining with baking paper and scoop the batter onto the tray, leaving a two-inch space to breathe to prevent fluffing up in the oven.

Bake at 180 degrees C (375 degrees F) for fifteen minutes to twenty minutes until the top part is lightly golden brown.

Enjoy!

Nutritional Information: 62 calorie; 5 g fat (2.4 g saturated fat); 101 mg cholesterol; 204 mg sodium; 0.6 g carbohydrate; 0 g dietary fiber; 0.2 g total sugars; 3.7 g protein.

KETO BREAD

Switching to a ketogenic diet could be difficult at first, especially if you are fond of carbohydrate-loaded foods, such as pastries, bread or pasta. But with this bread recipe, you can always eat less guilty as the recipe is vegetarian, Keto, Paleo, low carb, and gluten-free.

Servings: 16 slices

Ingredients

2 tablespoons **coconut oil**

½ cup **butter** melted

1 teaspoon **baking powder**

1/2 teaspoon **salt**

7 large **eggs**

1/2 teaspoon **xanthan gum**

2 cups **almond meal**

Directions

Preheat the oven at 180 degrees C (355 F).

Beat the eggs in a bowl for one to two minutes on high speed of your electric mixer.

Beat in melted butter and coconut oil and beat the remaining ingredients until the mixture has thickened, but easy to handle.

Prepare a loaf pan by lining with baking paper.

Serve!

Nutritional Information: 234 calorie; 23 g fat (14 g saturated fat); 1 g carbohydrate; 7 g protein.

KETO PUMPKIN BREAD – PSYLLIUM HUSK KETO BREAD

Impress your loved ones who adapt a ketogenic diet to lose weight. The pumpkin Keto bread is free of dairy, low carb, Keto, free of gluten and vegetarian. It is laxative due to the presence of psyllium husk, so perfect if you are suffering from irritable bowel syndrome or constipation.

Servings: 16 slices

Ingredients

1/3 cup **coconut flour**

1 cup **ground walnuts**

1/8 cups **erythritol**

1/4 cup **psyllium husk powder**

1/2 teaspoon **salt**

1 teaspoon **mixed spice** or **pumpkin spice**

1 teaspoon **baking powder**

5 large **eggs**

1/4 teaspoon **ginger**

3 ounces **pumpkin puree**

Note: Omit the ginger if using pumpkin spice.

Directions

Preheat the oven at 180 degrees C (355 F).

Combine all dry ingredients together in a large bowl.

Beat the pumpkin puree and eggs in a medium-size bowl with an electric mixer.

Gradually fold the dry ingredients into the egg-pumpkin mixture, stir to combine well.

Scrape the batter into your greased loaf tin pan.

Sprinkle on top with pumpkin seeds if desired.

Bake for forty-five minutes.

Enjoy!

Nutritional Information: 188 calorie; 14 g fat (9.5 g carbohydrate); 6.5 g dietary fiber; 7.2 g protein.

Low Carb Bread Mix

Your breakfast and brunch would be more nutritious if you prepare this bread mix more often. Each slice is dairy-free, gluten-free, low carb, ketogenic, nut-free, Paleo and vegetarian, so it won't make you fat and enjoy more than a slice of this moist and buttery bread.

Servings: 16 slices

Ingredients

1 teaspoon **baking powder**

2 cups **almond meal**

1/2 teaspoon **salt**

½ teaspoon **xanthan gum**

1¼ cups **water**

3 ounces **whole egg powder**

4 ounces (30 g) **butter**, room temperature

Directions

Preheat oven at 180 degrees C (355 F).

Combine in a large bowl the almond meal, baking powder, xanthan gum and 1/2 teaspoon salt, stir to combine well.

Combine in another bowl the butter, water and whole egg powder; pour mixture into the almond meal mixture and combine until incorporated.

Line the bottom of an 8 ½"by 4 ½" loaf tin pan with parchment paper and fill with the batter.

Level out the surface with spatula and bake for fifty minutes.

Remove from oven when the bread is done.

Let cool on wire rack before slicing into 12 to 16 slices.

Serve!

Nutritional Information: 137 calorie; 12.2 g fat (4.2 g saturated fat); 37 mg cholesterol; 149 mg sodium; 3.5 g carbohydrate; 1.5 g dietary fiber; 1.3 g total sugars; 4.7 g protein.

KETO SODA BREAD RECIPE

Enjoy unlimited slices of this flavorful Keto soda bread loaded with nutritional yeast flakes, ghee, apple cider vinegar, coconut flour, eggs, almond flour, baking soda, baking powder and sweetened with erythritol or stevia. The chia seeds give the bread a nutty texture.

Servings: 10 slices (1 loaf)

Ingredients

1 tablespoon **apple cider vinegar**

2 large **eggs**

1 1/2 tablespoons **nutritional yeast flakes**

2 tablespoons **ghee**

1/4 cup **coconut flour**

1 cup **almond flour**

1 teaspoon **baking soda**

3 tablespoons **ground chia seeds**

Dash of **erythritol** or **stevia** to taste

1 teaspoon **baking powder**

Pinch of **salt**

Directions

Preheat the oven at 350 degrees Fahrenheit (175 C).

Whisk in a bowl the eggs and vinegar together.

Whisk in melted ghee and nutritional yeast flakes until well blended.

Combine in a separate bowl the almond flour, coconut flour, ground chia seeds, baking soda, baking powder, erythritol or stevia, and a generous pinch of salt, until the mixture reaches fairly solid mass.

Place the batter onto a baking tray lined with a sheet of parchment paper.

Slightly flatten into a ball and create a design on top with a butter knife if desired.

Bake for twenty-five to thirty minutes until there is no more batter left on a cake tester.

Remove tray from oven; let cool completely. Slice and serve.

Enjoy!

Nutritional Information: 153 calorie; 2 g net carbs; 1 g total sugars; 12 g fat; 6 g carbohydrate; 4 g dietary fiber; 6 g protein.

NUT FREE 90 SECOND KETO BREAD - SESAME SEED KETO BREAD

Prepare Keto bread in ninety second only by combining the ingredients in a mug and microwave for 90 seconds. But if you want it cooked in the oven, bake it for fifteen minutes. This Keto, Paleo, nut free, low carb and gluten-free bread calls for sesame seed flour, so this makes this bread safe for people who are allergic to nuts and coconut.

Servings: 2 Keto bread mugs

Ingredients

1 large **egg**

1/4 cup **sesame seed flour**

1 teaspoon **baking powder**

1 tablespoon **butter**

1 pinch **salt**

Directions

Put together in a mug the baking powder and sesame seed flour and mix until well combined.

Add the egg, salt and butter to the mixture in a mug until incorporated.

Microwave for ninety seconds or bake in an oven for fifteen minutes.

Serve!

Nutritional Information: 250 calorie; 16 g fat; 3 g carbohydrate; 22 g protein.

CONGRATULATIONS!

YOU HAVE MADE IT TO THE END ! AS A TOKEN OF OUR
APPRECIATION PLEASE CLICK ON THE BOOK BELOW AND
ENTER YOUR EMAIL ADDRESS TO SUBSCRIBE TO OUR
NEWSLETTER & CLAIM YOUR FREE COOKBOOK!

Also, by the editors at Savour Press's kitchen

The Chili Cookbook

The Quiche Cookbook

Indian Instant Pot Cookbook

The Cajun and Creole Cookbook

The Grill Cookbook

The Burger Book

The Ultimate Appetizers Cookbook

The West African Cookbook

Korean Seoul Cookbook

The Cast Iron Cookbook

The Holiday Cookbook

The Baking Book

The Crepe Cookbook

BV

CONCLUSION

Thank you so much for downloading this eBook. We at Savour Press hope this book has increased your knowhow regarding some delicious and nutritious low carb Keto breads. This eBook contains a curated list of what we believe to be the 35 best Keto breads, which cover a variety of flavors, preparation and tastes. All different categories of Keto bread are represented such as your Keto flatbread, Keto cornbread, Keto sesame bread, Keto pumpkin bread, Keto cracker bread, Keto cloud bread, and many more. While in the thick preparation of these recipes, we came up with a consensus that every single ingredient should be easy to find and the instructions are concise, easy and simple, so that cooking newbies would not have a hired time applying what they have read. Each recipe does not use sugar as a sweetener and the flour is usually coconut flour, almond flour, arrowroot flour, and flax meal. Since Keto is non-dairy, it uses coconut milk instead with some ingredients to add more flavors. We hope you will enjoy cooking with these recipes.

Thanks again for your support.

Happy Cooking!

Made in the USA
Columbia, SC
09 May 2023

16242689R00055